Personal Computer Communications

Personal Computer Communications

Robert L. Perry

Franklin Watts
A Division of Grolier Publishing
New York • London • Hong Kong • Sydney
Danbury, Connecticut

To Brian Dolbeare, my resident computer genius and stepson

Note to readers: Definitions for words in **bold** can be found in the Glossary at the back of this book.

Photographs ©: Bill Frymire/MasterFile: 48; Earl Zubkoff Photography: 24; Monkmeyer Press: 8 (Kerbs); Noriko/Concept Images: 6, 46; petersonphotographics: cover; Photo Researchers: 51 (James King-Holmes/SPL); PhotoEdit: 44 top (Cindy Charles), 50 (Tony Freeman), 22 (Spencer Grant), 20 (Michael Newman), 11 top (Mark Richards); Steve Gottlieb Photography: 5 bottom, 14 (Steve Gottlieb); Stock Boston: 44 bottom (Peter Menzel), 34 (Eric Neurath), 25 (Robert Rathe), 5 top, 42 (Susan Van Etten); The Stock Market: 40 (Lester Lefkowitz); Tony Stone Images: 11 bottom (Phil Degginger).

Visit Franklin Watts on the Internet at: http://publishing.grolier.com

Library of Congress Cataloging-in-Publication Data

Perry, Robert L. (Robert Louis), 1950-
    Personal Computer Communicatons / by Robert L. Perry.
        p.   cm.— (Watts Library)
    Includes bibliographical references and index.
    Summary: Describes the workings of personal computers and how they can be connected to different kinds of networks, including the Internet.
    ISBN 0-531-11758-8 (lib. bdg.)   0-531-16483-7 (pbk)
    1. Microcomputers–Juvenile literature. [1. Microcomputers 2. Computer networks.] I. Title. II. Series.

QA76.23P462000   00-021380

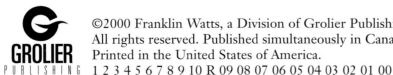

Contents

Chapter One
How a Personal Computer Communicates 7

Chapter Two
All About Modems 15

Chapter Three
How Computers Communicate with Each Other 21

Chapter Four
Internet Communication 35

Chapter Five
Communicating without Telephone Wires 41

Chapter Six
The Future: Internet Everywhere 47

53 **Glossary**

58 **To Find Out More**

60 **A Note on Sources**

61 **Index**

Computers connect people and information around the globe.

Chapter One

How a Personal Computer Communicates

Perhaps your teachers use personal computers (computers) to connect to the **Internet** so they can find interesting **World Wide Web** sites. Maybe they use personal computers to send electronic mail (e-mail) messages between schools.

They might even have the capacity to send and receive photographs or videos from computers in distant places.

Perhaps your parents use computers at their jobs to send e-mail to other people in their company or even to different parts of the world. They may use computers to access information from other computers thousands of miles away.

Maybe you already do all this yourself. Even if you do—and especially if you don't—do you understand how a personal computer can send e-mail, connect through the Internet to millions of websites, share information with other computers, and much more? That is, do you know how personal computers communicate?

Computers at school are usually connected through a network.

A Small Point in a Huge Network

When a personal computer sends and receives digital signals to another computer, it uses **data communications**. It acts as one point or **node** on a data communications **network**. Data communication involves transmitting digital information from one point to another with electrical signals through wires, cables, or airwaves.

With home-based computers, your node on a network would be your computer, which is almost always connected by using a telephone line. However, at your school or parents' workplace, the computers may be connected to other computers in several ways:

- By using a telephone line, like your computer at home
- By using a **Local Area Network** (LAN), a relatively small group of computers usually connected by electrical cables in one location
- By using a **Wide Area Network** (WAN), a much larger network that can connect hundreds or thousands of computers and LANs across a city, a country, or even the world

What LANs Do

A LAN gives connected computers the capability of communicating with each other along with sharing servers (central sites for software and information), printers, and other peripherals (devices connected to computers such as optical scanners).

Computers Have Connections

So, with one telephone line, your computer can share information with computers and networks around the world through a wide variety of connections. These connections may include normal telephone lines, **fiber-optic cables**, **microwave** transmitters (radio waves), **infrared** signals, television cables, and communication satellites. Here's how it works.

First, the signal travels from your computer's **modem** through the telephone lines to a central telephone office. From there, the signal may travel through the air across a regional microwave network or through a national fiber-optic cable network. Then, it may be sent into space and bounce off a communications satellite or travel under the ocean through a fiber-optic cable to Europe, Asia, or another continent. All this happens in mere seconds. The rest of this book discusses how all of these astonishing things are possible.

How Computers Can Communicate at All

Consider what a personal computer is and how it can send and receive signals from other computers. A personal computer consists of a **central processing unit** (CPU), primary memory (called random access memory or RAM), secondary memory (a floppy disk drive, a hard disk drive, and usually, a compact disc drive or CD-ROM), and various input/output (I/O) devices called **peripherals**.

Modern computers can run faster, but are smaller and take up less space than the computers made a few years ago.

Computer chips are getting smaller , but they are more powerful than ever before.

These I/O peripherals include the familiar keyboard and mouse (both input devices), the video monitor and printer (both output devices), and a special communications device for both input and output called a **modem**.

Inside your computer, these I/O devices are connected to the CPU or **microprocessor**. It is a single **semiconductor chip** that controls all of the basic computer operations. On this chip are

A Unique Pathway

Each peripheral, such as your keyboard, mouse, printer, floppy disk, hard drive, and CD-ROM, has a unique pathway with a different number of wires. Look at the back of your computer. You can see that each device uses different cable types and pin connectors.

thousands of **transistors**, pathways for electronic signals. They are divided into different groups—a control unit, basic memory, and an arithmetic logic unit. Each group controls a different aspect of the computer's operation.

The I/O peripherals connect to the CPU through an I/O bus. Like a real bus, the I/O bus carries signals along different electrical pathways among the microprocessor, memory chips, and different I/O devices.

Parallel Versus Serial Ports

A microprocessor can send many signals or **bits** (electric pulses) of digital information at a time. The Intel Pentium CPU, for example, can send 32 bits at a time through a pathway called a **port**. A port that can carry numerous bits at the same time is called a **parallel port**.

However, a computer can communicate through the telephone lines only in a very different way. It can send only one bit at a time through a **serial port**. Serial means in a series, single file, or one at a time.

It Wasn't That Long Ago

1945 ENIAC, with 18,000 vacuum tubes, became the first programmable calculator.

1947 Bell Laboratories invented the solid-state transistor, making the microprocessor possible years later.

1948 EDVAC was the first programmable computer with internal memory and programmable storage.

1971 The microprocessor was invented, launching the personal computer revolution.

A serial port carries one bit of information at a time (see above), while a parallel port sends lots of information at once (left). Computers communicate over the phone through a serial port, which is why the connection takes longer.

Compare parallel and serial ports to a kick-off at a football game. During the kickoff of a real game, the kicking team sends 11 players racing down the field together. They are running in parallel. A parallel port can send 8, 16, 32, 64, or even more signals rushing down a cable together. But a serial port can send only one bit or "player" down the cable at a time. The bits flow in a single file.

Kilobits and Megabits

Through years of creative work, telephone and computer engineers have figured out how to send—one at a time—tens of thousands of bits through the phone line each *second*. This rate is called **bits per second (bps)**: 1,000 bits per second is a **kilobit (Kbps)**. One million bits per second is called a **megabit (Mbps)**. So when you hear that a computer is communicating through its modem at 28.8 Kbps or 56Kbps, it means that it can send 28,800 or 56,000 bits of digital information per second. The fastest speed on a conventional modem at this time is 56K.

Currently, computers communicate with one another through the phone lines.

Chapter Two

All About Modems

To "communicate," a personal computer must first be connected to a network through a telephone line or direct network connection. A computer sends signals in digital bits. However, all traditional communication methods—phone lines, radio, television, and satellites—use **analog signals**. These signals fluctuate between a high and a low point and act like waves, which is also called a frequency.

The traditional telephone can send and receive analog signals in the narrow frequency range that people can hear—from 300 **hertz** (electrical waves) to 3,300 hertz per second. Yet, a digital computer can communicate at much faster speeds than 3,300 hertz.

A computer communicates by using digital bits, and cannot send these bits directly across an analog wire. They are two completely different types of signals. It would be like someone speaking English to someone who only speaks Chinese.

How a Modem Works

A computer needs a "translator" to send and receive signals across telephone networks. That translator is called a modem, short for MOdulator-DEModulator. When you send a signal over an analog line at speeds higher than 3,300 hertz, you also create problems that cause transmission mistakes. The signal can lose its strength and slow down, signals can cross, and other telephone lines can cause interference or noise.

A modem solves these problems. It translates the digital signals to fit the capacity or **bandwidth** of a normal telephone line with a method that is called modulation. Bandwidth is the

The modem translates the information between the computer and the phone line.

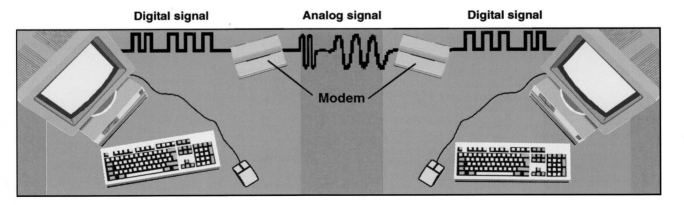

Digital signal   Analog signal   Digital signal

Modem

16

amount of data—number of digital bits—that can be sent through a communications line in one second.

Modulation means that at the computer, the first signal—digital bits—is changed into an analog signal. The signal is then sent across the telephone line. At the receiving end, the analog signal is changed back to its original digital state and read by the receiving computer. This is called demodulation.

Modem Methods

Modems can operate in three basic ways: simplex, half duplex, and full duplex. Simplex means only one-way transmission from one computer to another. Half duplex means that a computer can send and receive signals—two-way transmission—but not at the same time. And full duplex means that a computer can send and receive signals in both directions at the same time. All modern computer modems are full duplex modems.

Modern modems can send and receive information at the same time.

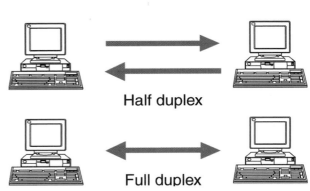

Simplex

Half duplex

Full duplex

With new methods to correct errors, modem makers increased modem speeds during the 1980s and 1990s steadily from 300 bps to 28.8 Kbps. An ordinary modem can send data at 56 Kbps, 187 *times* faster than just a few years ago, and many companies are continuing to develop faster methods of **broadband** data transmission.

A Modem with Every Computer

Today, almost every computer includes a modem with communication software that automatically dials the telephone. Called a modem card, internal, or external modem, it includes the entire modem device and its own memory and software, and it uses the computer's power supply.

During the past decade, **telecommunications** companies, those that manage telephone systems, have developed new types of digital communication devices that are replacing analog modems. These companies are replacing their traditional networks with purely digital ones that eliminate the need to translate digital signals to analog ones.

Computers That Send Faxes

Adding a modem to a computer allows you to do many new activities, not just the Internet. For example, you can use your computer as a **facsimile machine** or fax. With a fax, you can copy and transmit words, drawings, and images to another fax machine—even photographs and maps—anywhere in the world.

Super Fast Method

One digital communication method called ISDN (*integrated digital services network*) can transmit data from computers at up to 128 Kbps. In many areas, you can buy or rent special equipment and pay a monthly fee to the local telephone company for this service.

These new networks are creating a revolution in computer communications. But this remarkable change cannot happen unless there are enough high-capacity networks to manage the huge and increasing number of people who use the Internet, electronic mail, and similar services.

You may recognize these computers that check you out at a store.

Chapter Three

How Computers Communicate with Each Other

Computer networks are everywhere today—from your home computer to your school to a department store. They are as much a part of your daily life as

The Vast Internet Network

When you use a computer to link to the Internet, you may think it just calls another computer. What really happens is far more complex. First, when you start up your **web browser** (a special program that allows you to navigate through the Internet), a communications software program in your computer calls a host computer. The **Internet Service Provider** (ISP) you decide to use operates this host computer. The ISP's computer acts as a gateway offering you access to tens of thousands of other computers around the world.

When you enter a web address (unique numbers or letters that identify a specific location on the web), you tell your ISP's host computer to send a message looking for that page. That message may go through thousands of computer networks before it finds the right one.

Internet Service Providers have rooms full of computers whose sole responsibility is to connect you to other computers.

automobiles and televisions. If you've ever watched a credit card purchase processed in a store, you've seen them use a computer network. The store clerk slides the card through a card reader, actually a simple computer, that reads the account information on the stripe on the back of the card. The reader then calls a host computer at a bank that could be hundreds of miles away.

The bank computer answers the phone, receives the credit card number and amount of the sale, checks the credit card to make sure it's okay, and returns a signal approving the sale. The process takes only a few seconds. How? By using the power, speed, and capacity of the computer network.

What Is a Computer Network?

A computer network is a group of computers and smart peripherals. They are linked through a variety of communication links, including telephone lines, fiber-optic cables, cable television cables, radio (or microwave) transmitters, and satellites. Each connection works at a different speed, which means that it can transmit different amounts of data per second.

Any link that transmits at less than 1 Mbps is called **narrowband.** Broadband or high-speed connections can transmit at much higher speeds, for example:

- Co-axial cable, like your TV cable, from 1 to 3 Mbps
- Fiber-optic cable, from 10 to 100 Mbps
- Microwaves, from 1 to 45 Mbps and higher

Fast Phone Communications

A new type of modem called an asynchronous digital subscriber line (ADSL) modem can send signals over regular phone lines at more than 1 *million bits per second,* 25 times faster than a 56Kbps modem.

Fiber-optic technology, which uses light transmission, will make it possible for faster speeds on phone lines.

- Satellites, from 1.5 Mbps to billions of bits per second (**gigabits** or Gbps)

More Speed, More Data at Lower Prices

As people want faster links to the Internet, communications companies are laying more fiber-optic lines, adapting TV cables for digital data, building more microwave transmitters, and launching more satellites.

The price of connecting to computer networks is falling lower, too. For example, you can get free or low-cost access to the Internet through your school. Or you can gain free access through public libraries or directly to your home for $10 a month in some areas.

Having Your Network Cake and Eating It, Too

To understand how networks work, you can compare a computer network to a chocolate layer cake with two layers of cake, a layer of filling, and some delicious frosting. Networks are stacked in the same way, but each layer has a different function so all of the layers can work together.

Working from the inside of the network to the outside, here are the layers and what they do:

Microwave towers provide faster services through direct transmissions.

- **Physical**—The first layer includes the physical hardware: computers, modems, cables, host computers, telephone lines, and so on.

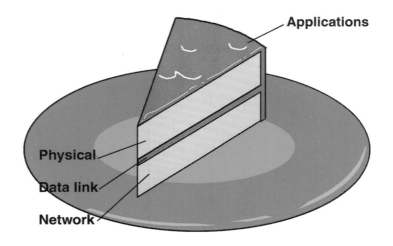

A network works something like a cake with layers of transmission.

- **Data link**—The "filling" controls how the information is sent across the physical layer and detects and corrects errors.
- **Network**—The second layer translates the computer message into one that the network can understand, and it decides which path or route to use.
- **Applications**—The "frosting" is the all-important layer that you work with when you use an electronic mail software, Internet browser, or communication program.

Each message must travel through all four layers at both ends. All four layers of each computer must be compatible, which means that they must be able to understand or translate the signals from the other computers. If they don't, your message cannot go through.

LANs and WANS

Personal computers often are connected in a school or business through a Local Area Network or LAN. A LAN is a system that links from as few as two, to as many as hundreds of computers. Schools and businesses use LANs for two main reasons:

- To allow users to share the same information and files, swap e-mail messages, and link to the Internet.

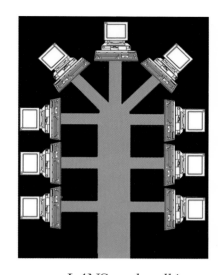

LANS work well in schools or businesses where computers are physically close to one another.

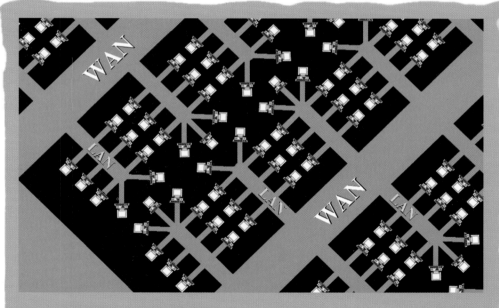

The Largest WAN of All

A WAN links a LAN to the outside world. The Internet can be considered a massive WAN that links WANS and LANS together.

- To share the same software and peripherals, such as file servers and printers.

However, a LAN is used to share information and resources with computers that are physically close to each other, like in the same building. When a school or business needs to link to the outside world, it often requires a connection to a much larger network, such as a Wide Area Network or WAN. A WAN links LANs together across great distances, from across a large city to even around the world.

Types of Local Area Networks

There are two basic types of LANs: 1) **client-server network** and 2) **peer-to-peer network**. A client-server network dedicates a computer to manage communication with other computers, files, and peripherals. This server computer acts like both a servant and a boss to the other computers on the same network. It serves them by allowing access to shared files and programs, but it manages them by controlling what they can use.

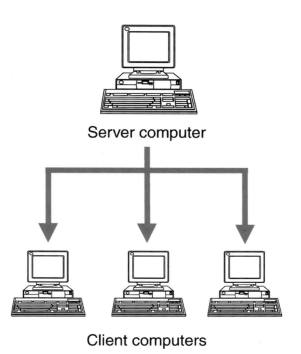

Server computer

Client computers

There are two types of LAN networks: client-server and peer-to-peer.

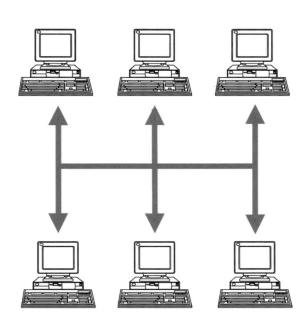

Peer-to-peer network

In a peer-to-peer network, each computer acts like a server to the other computers—its peers—and a client. Any computer can request and receive information and programs at any time from any other computer. A peer-to-peer LAN often runs more slowly than a client-server network, so that most larger LANs use the client-server type.

How LANs Work

Both types of LANs work in the same general way. Each computer is connected to a main cable with a network card installed on the computer. This card and specific network communication software allows the computer to communicate in the same "language" that the network router uses. A network operating system (a group of programs) manages the LAN and how it works with its computers and peripherals.

Information flows around a LAN very quickly. To manage these rapid flows and make sure all users receive the data and programs they need when they need it, companies have developed several **typologies**, or network layouts: **Ethernet**, **token ring**, and **star**.

The Ethernet Tree

An Ethernet LAN works like a tree with branches sticking out of it. Each branch or point—which means the computer, server, or peripheral—has an adapter and a unique address. The adapter sends a message in both directions around the

LAN. Each computer on the network inspects each message as it zooms by and ignores it if that computer's address is not in the message. If the address is there, the receiving computer reads the message and returns a "thank you" message to the sender.

The Token Ring Carousel

The token ring typology works more like an unusual carousel at the fair. On a normal carousel, *you* ride the wooden horse and try to grab a brass ring as you go by. In a token ring LAN, the *brass ring*, called a token, rides around the network, and the computers grab it as it goes by.

This token constantly goes around and around the network loop. Each computer's adapter can identify the ring. When you want to send a message, your computer waits until the token goes by, grabs it, adds its message, and sends the token and the message around the LAN to its destination.

The Star Wheel

The star network works more like the spokes on a wheel. Each computer has its own spoke or line that connects to a central hub, the server. The hub has switches that can link any computer to any other computer or more than one computer on the network.

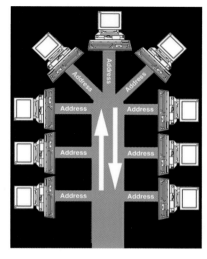

An Ethernet tree takes a look at a message and retrieves it if it is meant for that particular computer.

The token ring acts like a carousel, grabbing the token when necessary.

31

The star network is useful for avoiding data collisions.

A computer sends a message with the address of the destination computer to the hub. The hub opens the switch and routes the message to the intended computer. By opening and closing switches at different times, the hub avoids data collisions.

How Backbones and WANs Work

LANs are often connected to other LANs through backboned networks. A backbone uses very high speeds to manage huge amounts of information flowing through the network. To understand how a LAN, a backbone, and a WAN work together, imagine a city water system. Your house has a small water pipe, so only a small amount of water can flow through it at a time. A computer connection through a telephone line is like that small pipe because only a relatively small amount of information can flow through that line.

But the pipe under the street that carries water to all the houses in your neighborhood is much wider than the one in your house. It carries a lot more water that moves at much higher speeds. Likewise, a LAN can carry many times more information much faster than a single computer connection.

That pipe under your street is connected to an even larger pipe that carries water from the city treatment plant to your neighborhood. Likewise, a backbone connects many LANs and can carry huge amounts of data.

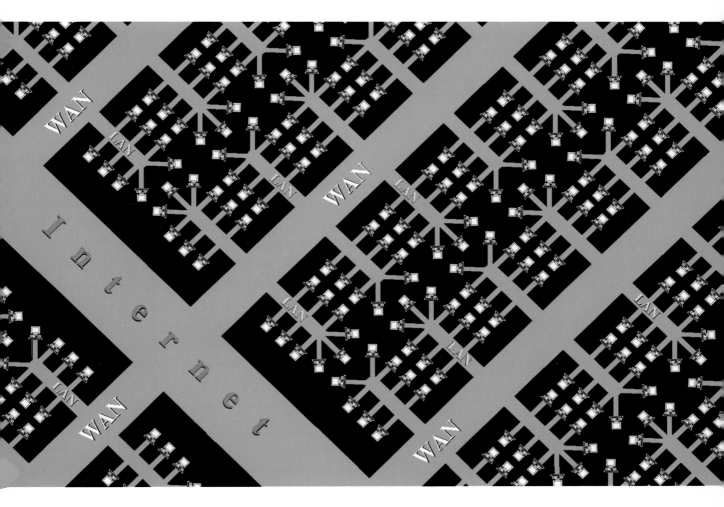

Largest of all, the pipe that carries water from the reservoir to your city may be huge and carry thousands of gallons per minute. WANs work like these huge water pipes and carry tens, even hundreds of millions and billions of bits per second.

So, LANs, WANs, and backbones make it possible for your computer to communicate quickly, cheaply, and accurately across the world through electronic mail and the Internet.

Backboned networks enable a lot of information to travel all at once.

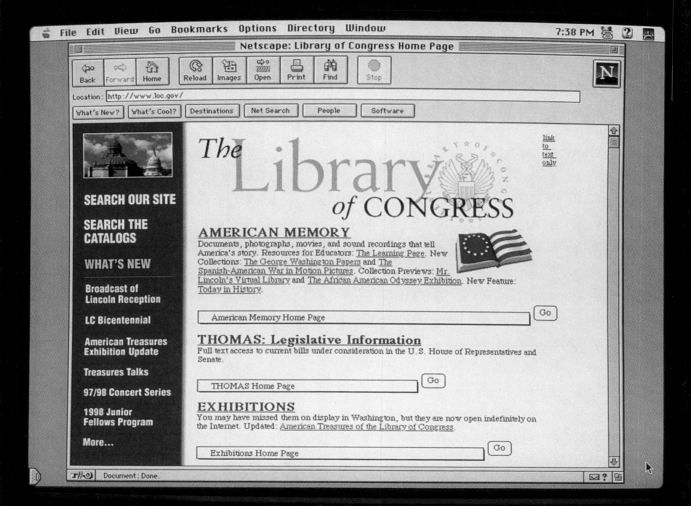

The Internet enables you to connect to a wide variety of sites to find lots of interesting information. Here is the Library of Congress site.

Chapter Four

Internet Communication

The Internet is rapidly changing many things about how you learn, play, find information, and even communicate with your friends. Your access to these services begins with your computer. To communicate across the Internet, first, you start your web browser software that calls on the computer's communication software, which tells your computer's modem to connect to your Internet Service Provider (ISP). Your ISP could be a local company, a telecommunications firm, a school or university, or an **information provider.** After the connection is established, your web browser begins to receive and display the Internet "Address" or "Location" requested.

What's in a URL?

In this area, you type the **Universal Resource Locator** (URL) address of the website you want to reach. URLs are designed so that the user can easily remember the desired host computer or site. A URL can be broken into three parts. The first part identifies what the site is designed to offer. "WWW" and "FTP" are some examples commonly found in URLs. "WWW" stands for World Wide Web. URLs that begin with "www" identify that the site is accessed through the World Wide Web. If the URL begins with "ftp," which stands for File Transfer Protocol, the site is designed to transfer specific files that the user might want to receive or retrieve.

The second part of the URL identifies the site's unique name. These names are picked by the host to identify them from other sites. Examples of sites might include: *www.apple.com* (Apple Computers) or *www.fema.gov* (Federal Emergency Management Agency). A period, or what is commonly called a dot, separates each part of the URL. The last part of a URL identifies the top-level domain that the site resides under. Examples of these include: .com, which stands for commercial; .edu, which represents an educational unit; or .gov, which stands for government. As the Internet grows, so does the list of URLs.

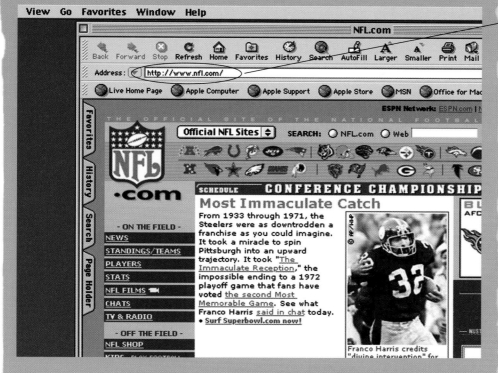

This is an example of a URL

URLs

The six parts of a URL include the following:

- *http* tells you that the site is on the World Wide Web and uses a computer language called *hypertext mark-up language* (HTML).
- *://* symbols tell your browser that the next words and symbols will be the actual address.
- *www.* (followed by a period or "dot") shows that the address you want is on the World Wide Web.
- *domain name* (followed by a "dot") is the unique site name.
- *top-level domain* indicates either the purpose of the site (*.com* for business, *.gov* for government, *.org* for non-profit, and so on) or the country where the site is located. For example, the top-level domain *.uk* means that the site is located in the United Kingdom in Europe.
- *pages* (after each backslash / mark) are the specific file or page locations. For example, *http://www.nfl.com/teams* leads you to the NFL's page that leads to all the teams in the league.

What's in a Domain Name?

When you enter the URL into the address space and press Return (or Enter), your browser sends a request through your modem to the nearest node for the Domain Name System (DNS). The DNS is an addressing service or white pages that your computer uses for the Internet. Each top-level domain (.com, .edu, etc.) has primary servers that track and respond to requests, as do second-level domains (like microsoft.com or duke.edu). Each DNS contains resources, addresses, and locations that identify the actual address of a specific computer host on the Internet. The DNS lists every unique numbered address for each website, called an Internet Protocol (IP) or TCP/IP address.

The DNS sends the site's unique TCP/IP address back to your browser. Computers communicate faster by using numbers instead of words, so when you want to view a specific site or page, your browser first calls upon a local DNS server to translate the URL into a specific TCP/IP address. A TCP/IP address might look something like this: 199.0.10.112. Just like you dial an area code and number on your telephone, your browser needs the correct computer address, or it will not be able to connect you to the site or web page you desire. After the DNS server gives your browser the exact address, it can contact and establish a connection with the proper host computer. After establishing this connection, the browser begins to retrieve, download, and translate the website. By translating this information, your browser provides you with the page the way the author intended you to view it.

Connecting to the web opens doors to millions of interesting, exciting, and fun sites. You can find everything from online adventure games to information that can help you succeed in school. You can also find kid-safe chat rooms where you can swap e-mail messages and make new friends in different cities, states, and countries.

In the future, computers will probably be connected to one another through satellites.

Chapter Five

Communicating Without Telephone Wires

Today, most computers communicate through telephone lines, a set of copper wires that lead from the computer to a telephone pole on the street. But, in some homes and many companies today—and maybe at your house within a few years—computers may be connected by a variety of other communication methods.

Wireless laptops will enable computers to communicate without connecting directly to a phone line.

Get Mobile with Wireless

An infrared transmitter works just like the remote control on your television: it sends pulses of light with high-speed digital signals across the invisible red spectrum. However, just as you have to point the remote control at your TV, your computer has to be in the line of sight of the infrared signal.

A radio transmitter can send digital waves that can pass through walls, so many businesses use wireless laptop computers. They allow employees to move from place to place inside a building, yet still connect to a LAN. For example, at Grandview Hospital in Dayton, Ohio, medical staff members carry wireless laptops around the hospital and communicate with the hospital's network. Each LAN has a wireless hub so the staff can access patient information from anywhere in the hospital.

Microwaves and Satellites Boost Bandwidth

Many companies also use satellite networks and microwave transmissions to communicate across a city or around the world. Very high-speed radio signals transmit thousands of computer data at a time. Ground-based microwave systems can send signals up to 1 billion bits per second (gigabits or Gbps). Satellites can transmit at speeds up to 30 Gbps, 30 times faster than a microwave system.

Both systems have interesting drawbacks. First, microwaves can send signals only in a straight line, so a series of in–line towers must boost the signals across the area. Another disadvantage is that bad weather can interfere with the signal.

Likewise, a satellite has to remain in a fixed position relative to the earth, called geosynchronous orbit. From there, a satellite receives a signal sent from one spot on earth, boosts the signal, and sends it back to another spot or region. In fact, some satellite TV services already offer computer communications and Internet links.

Hooking Computers to Cable TV

Competing with satellite TV, modern digital cable TV can send up to 500 channels, including TV programs, radio broadcasts, and computer signals at high speeds between 100 and 350 *times* faster than the common 56 Kbps telephone modem.

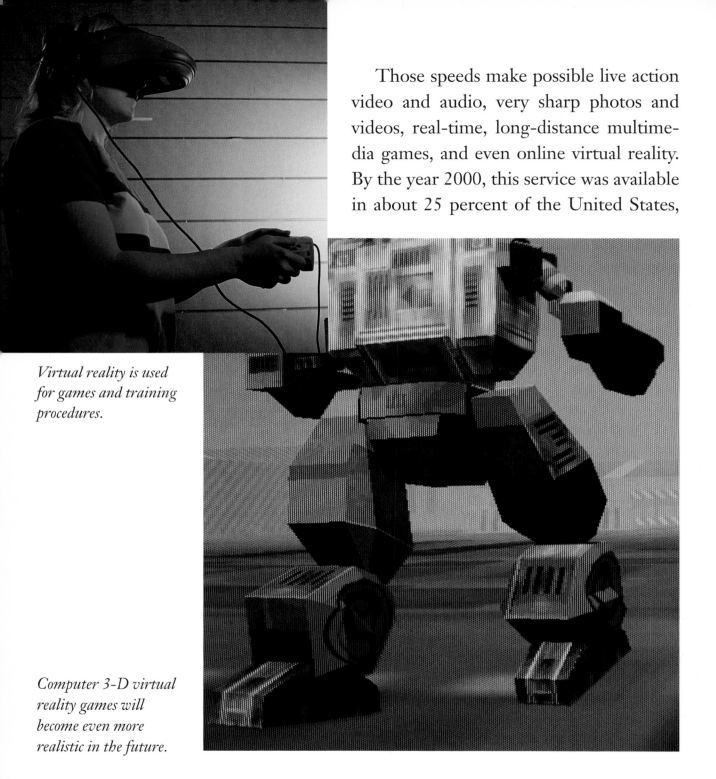

Those speeds make possible live action video and audio, very sharp photos and videos, real-time, long-distance multimedia games, and even online virtual reality. By the year 2000, this service was available in about 25 percent of the United States,

Virtual reality is used for games and training procedures.

Computer 3-D virtual reality games will become even more realistic in the future.

but cable companies are rapidly expanding this service, especially in major cities.

Fast Fiber-Optic Cables

A fiber-optic cable is faster than either TV cable or microwaves, but not as fast as the best satellite systems. Transmitting at speeds up to 2.4 Gbps, a fiber-optic cable could send the contents of the entire *Grolier Encyclopedia* in less than one second. These cables are now used to send thousands of phone calls and digital signals underground across the country and under the oceans from continent to continent, and they will be used even more often in the future.

Within a few years, your family may have a small microwave or satellite dish attached to your house or fiber-optic cable leading to your home. Either the dish or the cable will be the gateway for all of your telephone, computer, TV, and radio communications. These and similar services promise to create a revolution in computer communications.

In the future,
everyone may
communicate by
using a satellite dish.

Chapter Six

The Future: Internet Everywhere

If you have surfed the Internet, you haven't seen anything yet. The future of computer communications *is* the Internet. It is becoming a global electronic city where you can do just about anything through your home computer, your TV, even a wireless pocket computer that combines computer power with a telephone, e-mail, voice mail,

Internet access, and much more. All of the personal computer functions—text, data, audio, video, graphics, and multimedia—are converging into one gigantic network.

Global Networks Boom

By 2002, a network of 600 low-orbit satellites called the Teledesic system will circle the earth and make high-speed Internet access available anywhere to everyone with a computer. Tens of thousands of miles of fiber-optic cable are crisscrossing the oceans and connecting the continents. These new communications networks must be built to solve the most

Satellites in space will enable us to communicate anywhere with anyone at a moment's notice.

serious problem facing the Internet: the shortage of bandwidth, that is, the lack of enough capacity to carry the skyrocketing number of messages that travel the Internet every day.

Everywhere, Everything, Anytime Internet Access

Within 10 years, more than one *billion* people—one of every six people in the world—will use the Internet. They will connect with everything from desktop computers linked to normal telephone lines to computer wristwatch phones using satellites.

Even your family car may have a computer built into its dashboard. In 1998, Microsoft introduced the $1,000 auto computer with an AM/FM stereo, CD player and digital audio, e-mail, pager, and traffic alerts. Hand-held global satellite communicators with built-in antennas allow you to send e-mail from anywhere in the world, literally across oceans, jungles, or deserts.

Even at home, the Internet may be everywhere. Your family's desktop computer will still have its Internet connection, but so may your cable TV box, refrigerator, heating and cooling system, security alarm system, and lights.

When you're away from home, you and your family may carry wireless computers custom-made to fit the way you live. You could have your own hand-held unit that includes a cellular phone, voice mail, pager, e-mail, games, and basic com-

You're used to hand-held games, but in the future, you'll be able to access any kind of information you want from a tiny computer that fits in your hand.

puter functions. You could surf the web, do your homework, play games, and call, page, or e-mail your friends.

In fact, the Internet itself may become a vast intelligent network with "softbots" roaming the billions of web pages to find and analyze information. Intelligent "librarians" that talk may answer any question you ask and give you the answer by voice, text, data, graphs, audio, photos, or video streams.

Your Web-Based World

In short, you will live through the web, and you will be surrounded by the web in everything you do. To list just a few possibilities, you'll be able to do the following things:

- Download and save music to create your own compact discs.
- Download videos—with text and photos and graphics if you want—onto DVDs (digital video disks).
- Play interactive games with others around the world.
- Get answers to your homework questions from "softbots," intelligent programs that search the Internet for information.
- Do live videoconferences with other kids around the world.

Video phones will enable you to talk on the phone and see the person who is talking to you.

- Shop for books, clothes, toys, games, gifts, clothes, and software.

The key to all this will be the very high-speed connections that link all these computers to the Internet. Your desktop computer may still be linked to a phone line, but more likely to cable TV, a satellite network, a fiber-optic cable, or a wireless microwave system, perhaps all four. The computers in your parents' car may use wireless radio or satellite networks. Your pocket computer may use a wireless satellite or cellular phone network.

One thing is for sure: The Internet and the awesome communications network behind it will become the center of the daily lives of tens of millions of people.

The Future Super Computer

Computing power doubles every 18 months, so computers are always becoming faster with more powerful processing capacity and greater storage capacity. By 2005, the common computer will have not just 32 Mb of memory, but hundreds of millions of megabytes. It will run at speeds faster than 1 Gbps, store almost 1 trillion bytes (terabytes) on its hard drive, and include both super high-capacity CD-ROM and DVD (digital video disc) players.

Glossary

Analog signals—actual electrical waves that fluctuate between a high point and a low point (also called a frequency)

Bandwidth—the capacity of a communication line to carry electrical signals; **broadband** means that a line carries more than 1 million bits per second; **narrowband** refers to any line that carries less than 1 million bits per second

Bit—an electrical pulse that is sent across a communication medium (a **Kilobit** (Kbps) equals 1,000 bits per second; a **Megabit** (Mbps) equals 1 million bits per second; a **Gigabit** (Gbps) equals one billion bits per second; a **byte** is equal to eight bits)

Central Processing Unit (CPU)—the heart of a microcomputer where all primary computing functions take place

Client-server network—a group of computers in which one computer, the server, stores programs and files and manages the communication of the other computers

Data communications—the exchange of information between one computer and another through a communication line

Ethernet—a tree-like structure typology linking computers to a server

Facsimile machine—a machine that uses special electrical signals to copy images and transmit them across telephone lines (called a "fax," for short)

Fiber-optic cable—a communication line made of glass fibers that can send signals at very high speeds

Hertz (Hz.)—the measure of electrical or radio waves transmitted through a communication medium

Information provider—a company, such as America Online, that gathers useful information and services and offers access to them for a fee

Infrared—invisible light rays just beyond the red end of the spectrum used to send computer signals

Internet—a huge number of computers around the world linked together so they can share messages and information

Internet service provider (ISP)—a company that offers access to Internet information and services

Local Area Network (LAN)—a relatively small group of computers linked in a small area, such as an office building

Microprocessor—a single semiconductor chip that controls all basic computer operations

Modem—a device that translates analog telephone signals into digital signals so computers can communicate with traditional methods, such as telephone lines

Microwave—a short wave, usually less than one meter (1.0936 yards) long, used to transmit all kinds of electrical signals

Network—a group of computers connected to share programs and information

Node—a communications access point on a network, such as a computer or printer

Parallel port—transmits all signals at the same time

Peer-to-peer network—a group of computers in which each

computer can store information and share programs with all other computers in the same group

Peripherals—any input or output (I/O) device connected to a computer, such as a printer, a scanner, a keyboard, a monitor, and so on

Port—an access point through which a peripheral can be connected to the central processor

Semiconductor chip—a thumbnail-sized device with thousands of tiny transistors that perform computer operations

Serial port—sends each signal one at a time

Star—hub-and-spokes typology or structure linking computers to a server

Telecommunications—any communication across a long distance through telephones, radio waves, and so on

Token ring—a type of typology that sends a token or identifier in a constant loop around a network

Transistor—a very small electrical device that acts as a pathway for signals in, through, and out of a computer and its components

Typology—a type of local area network

Universal Resource Locator (URL)—the address of a web page and how a computer finds a page on the web

Web browser—a program that reads files written in HyperText Markup Language (HTML) so the files can be downloaded from the Internet and displayed on a monitor with formatted text, pictures, graphics, sound, or video

Wide Area Network (WAN)—connects a large number of computers and LANs across a large geographic area, such as a region, a state, a country, even the world

World Wide Web (WWW)—a huge collection of files stored on tens of thousands of computers connected to the Internet around the world that can be accessed with a computer and web browser.

To Find Out More

Books

Claiborne, Anna. *The Usborne Computer Dictionary for Beginners*. Tulsa, OK: EDC Publications, 1996.

Cochrane, Kerry. *The Internet*. New York: Franklin Watts, 1997.

Gardner, Robert. *Communication: Yesterday's Science, Today's Technology*. New York: Twenty-First Century Books, 1995.

Lampton, Christopher. *The World Wide Web*. New York: Franklin Watts, 1997.

Nimersham, Jack. *The First Book of Modem Communications*. Carmel, IN: Sams, 1991.

Stephens, Margaret, Treays, Rebecca, and Wingate, Phillip. *Computers for Beginners*. Tulsa, OK: EDC Publications, 1998.

White, Ron. *How Computers Work* (Deluxe Edition). Emeryville, CA: Ziff-Davis Press, 1997.

World Wide Web Sites

Kids and Computers
www.kidsandcomputers.com
This is a commercial site that offers information and education about computers and has links to numerous related sites.

Kidlink
www.kidlink.org
This group organizes and manages safe chat rooms for children around the world.

4Kids Org
www.4kids.org
You'll find an educational site here with links to many other educational sites, including those that teach about computers and programming.

A Note on Sources

Personal computer communication concerns many basic ideas about how computers operate. Many current popular books for children avoid these issues and focus on the fun aspects of "surfing" the Internet. However, you may want to understand the basics of computer communications so you know the complex process that takes place when you use your personal computer to access the Internet or send electronic mail. Without many resources aimed at middle-school children, I turned to numerous basic books for adults and my earlier work on computers. You may also find age-specific encyclopedias helpful to learn more details about interesting ideas, such as telecommunications, satellite transmission, microwaves, infrared light waves, and so on.

Index

Numbers in *italics* indicate illustrations.

ADSL (asynchronous digital subscriber line), 23
analog signals, 15–16, 53

backbone, 32–33, *33*
bandwidth, 16–17, 53
bits, 12, 53
broadband, 18, 23, 53
byte, 53

cables, 11
cable TV, 43–45
chips, *11*, 11–12
client-server network, 28, *29*, 53
co-axial cable, 23
communicating through phone lines, *14*
computer chips, *11*
computer connections, 9–10
CPU (central processing unit), 10, 53

data communications, 9, 54
data link layer, 26
digital bits, 16
DNS (Domain Name System), 38
domain name, 37, 38–39

EDVAC, 12
ENIAC, 12
Ethernet, 30, 54
Ethernet tree, 30–31, *31*
external modem, 18
facsimile machine, 18, 54
faxes, 18
fiber-optic cables, 10, 23, 45, 54
fiber–optic technology, *24*
frequency, 15
FTP (File Transfer Protocol), 36
full duplex modems, 17

Gbps (gigabits), 24, 53
geosynchronous orbit, 43
global networks, 48–49
Grolier Encyclopedia, 45

half duplex modems, 17
hand-held computers, *50*
hand-held global satellite
    communicators, 49
hertz (hz.), 16, 54
Hertz, Heinrich, 16
high-speed connections, 23
host computer, *22*
HTML (HyperText Mark-
    up Language), 37
HTML (HyperText Markup
    Language), 57
hub, 31–32
Hz. (hertz), 16, 54

information provider, 36, 54
infrared, 10, 54
infrared transmitter, 43
intelligent librarians, 50
internal modem, 18
Internet, 7, *22*, *27*, 35, 38,
    47–48, 54
Internet access, *25*, 49–50
I/O bus, 12
IP (Internet Protocol), 38

ISDN (integrated digital
    services network), 19
ISPs (Internet Service
    Providers), *22*, 35–36,
    55

Kbps (kilobit), 13, 53
keyboard, 11
Kidlink site, 59
Kids and Computers site, 59

LANs (Local Area
    Networks), 9, *27*, 27–32,
    30, 55
Library of Congress site,
    34
Mbps (megabit), 13, 53
memory, 10
microprocessor, 11, 12, 55
microwave dish, 45
microwaves, 10, 23, 55
microwave towers, *25*
microwave transmissions,
    43
modem card, 18
modem operations, 16–18
modems, 11, *16*, 17, 18, 55
modern computers, *11*
modulation, 16–17
mouse, 11

narrowband, 23, 53
network connections, 15, 23
network layer, 26
network layers, 25–26, *26*
networks, 9, 12, 23–24, 55
nodes, 9, 55

parallel ports, 12–13, 55
peer-to-peer network, 28,
    29, 30, 55–56
peripherals, 9, 10–11, 56
pin connectors, 11
ports, 12–13, 56
printer, 11

radio transmitter, 43
RAM (random access
    memory), 10

satellite connections, *40*
satellite dish, 45, *46*
satellite networks, 43
satellites, 48, *48*
school computers connected
    through network, *8*
second-level domains, 38
semiconductor chip, 11–12,
    56
serial ports, 12–13, *13*, 56
simplex modems, 17

solid-state transistor, 12
store computers, *20*
super computers, 52

TCP/IP address, 38
telecommunications, 56
telecommunications compa-
    nies, 18
Teledesic system, 48
token, 31
token ring, 30, *31*, 56
top-level domain, 36, 37
transistors, 12, 56
typology, 30, 57

URLs (Universal Resource
    Locators), 36–38, *37*, 57

video phones, *51*
virtual reality, *44*
virtual reality games, *44*

WANs (Wide Area
    Networks), 9, *27*, 28,
    32–33, 57
web address, 22
web browser, 22, 57
wireless laptops, 42
WWW (World Wide Web),
    7, 36, 37, 50-52, 57

About the Author

Noted author Robert L. Perry has written about personal computers for more than 20 years. He wrote one of the first books about microcomputers for home use and has authored several other books about computers and computer-related careers for Franklin Watts, including *Computer Crime* and *Electronic Service Careers*. He teaches professional writing at the University of Maryland, College Park, has a master's degree in speech communication, and makes his home near Annapolis, Maryland.